please!

JANINE AMOS

CHERRYTREE
BOOKS

A CHERRYTREE BOOK

This edition first published in 2005
by Cherrytree Books, part of
The Evans Publishing Group Limited
2A Portman Mansions
Chiltern Street
London W1U 6NR

© Evans Brothers Limited 2005

Printed in Italy

British Library Cataloguing in Publication data.

Amos, Janine
Please!. – (Good Manners)
1. Interpersonal relations – Juvenile literature
I. Title II. Spenceley, Annabel
395.1'22

ISBN 1 84234 376 9
13 digit ISBN (from January 2007) 978 1 84234 376 0

CREDITS
Editor: Louise John
Designer: Mark Holt
Photography: Gareth Boden
Production: Jenny Mulvanny

Based on the original edition of *Please!* published in 1998

With thanks to:
Genna and Karen Heron,
Harry Foster, Montel Adams,
Gareth, Annie, Lilly and Murray Boden

Monty's Ball

Murray kicks the ball.

4

It goes into Mr Boden's garden.

5

7

Mr Boden throws it back.

8

How is Monty feeling?

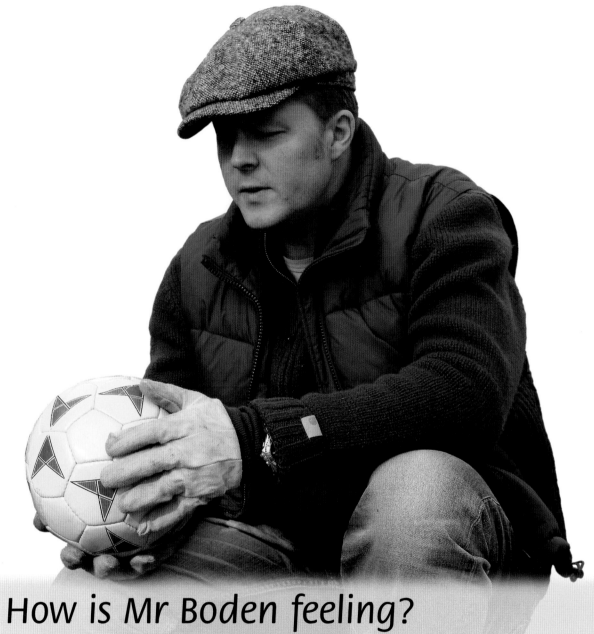

How is Mr Boden feeling?

Please may I have the ball back?

12

Monty tries again.

How does Mr Boden feel now?

13

14

Harry's Juice

16

Harry can't reach the juice.
Genna can.

No,
I won't.

17

Why won't Genna help Harry?
How does she feel?

Harry thinks about it.
What could he do?

19

A Story for Lilly

Lilly is tired.

I want another story.

22

How does Lilly feel?
How does her mum feel?

Lilly looks at her book and waits.

Mum drinks her coffee.

Then she reads Lilly a story.

28

Thank you,
Mum.

Most people are glad to help if they are asked.

30

But they don't like being told what to do.

TEACHER'S NOTES

By reading these books with young children and inviting them to answer the questions posed in the text the children can actively work towards aspects of the PSHE and Citizenship curriculum.

Develop confidence and responsibility and making the most of their abilities by
- recognising what they like and dislike, what is fair and unfair and what is right and wrong
- to share their opinions on things that matter to them and explain their views
- to recognise, name and deal with their feelings in a positive way

Develop good relationships and respecting the differences between people
- to recognise how their behaviour affects others
- to listen to other people and play and work co-operatively
- to identify and respect the differences and similarities between people

By using some simple follow up and extension activities, children can also work towards

Citizenship KS1
- to agree and follow rules for their group and classroom, and understand how rules help them

EXTENSION ACTIVITY
Rule of the week
- Introduce the children to the notion of a 'rule of the week' – a new rule that everyone must make a special effort to use. It may say something like 'Always say please when you are asking for something.'
- Read through the stories in *Please!* helping the children to identify the reasons why people say please and the feelings that not being asked politely may arouse.
- Ask the children to think of an example where they might want to ask for something and use the word please. Things such as 'Can I have some more, please?' or 'Can I sit there, please?' These sentences can be written on strips of paper and stuck on the 'rule of the week' board.
- On the rule of the week board write each child's name under the heading 'I have used the rule of the week today'. At the end of the day ask each child if they have used the rule of the week and when. If they have used the rule they may place a tick next to their name. (All children will receive a tick whenever possible.)
- Let lunchtime staff and parents know about the rule of the week so they can also provide reinforcement and praise.

These drama activities can be repeated on subsequent days with the other two stories in the book or with other stories from the series.